GEOGRAPHY OF THE US
MIDWEST STATES
(ILLINOIS, INDIANA, MICHIGAN, OHIO AND MORE)

GEOGRAPHY FOR KIDS
US STATES | 5TH GRADE SOCIAL STUDIES

BABY PROFESSOR
EDUCATION KIDS

Speedy Publishing LLC
40 E. Main St. #1156
Newark, DE 19711
www.speedypublishing.com

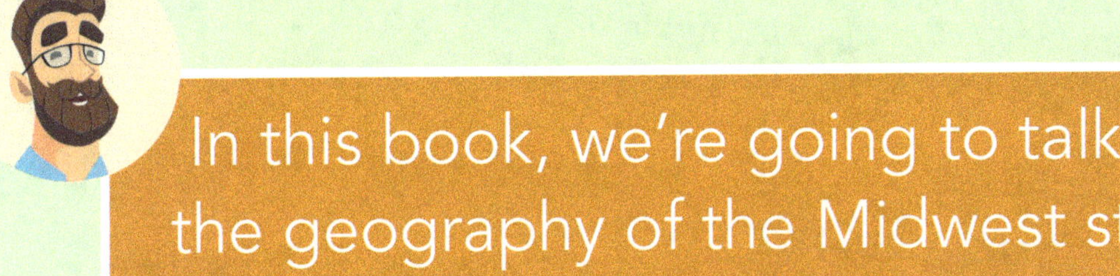
In this book, we're going to talk about the geography of the Midwest states of the United States. So, let's get right to it!

The Midwest section of the United States has fertile farmland and wide expanses of flat grasslands. The Mississippi River, one of the longest rivers in the world, winds its way through the Midwestern states. The Great Lakes are another important geographical feature of the Midwest.

MISSISSIPPI RIVER

RED RIVER VALLEY

NORTH DAKOTA

The state of North Dakota has several different types of topography. The eastern border is characterized by the Red River Valley. Perfect for agriculture, this fertile region of land was once underneath a glacier lake. To the west of this valley is the Drift Prairie region. It covers a large portion of the eastern section of the state. Its many gentle, rolling hills are separated by lakes and valleys.

BADLANDS NATIONAL PARK

The western section of the state is covered by the Great Plains region. It's broken by the state's most important river, the Missouri. In the southwest portion of this region are the Badlands. This long, narrow band of terrain has many unusual rock formations.

SYLVAN LAKE

SOUTH DAKOTA

The eastern portion of South Dakota is covered by the Central Lowlands, which include two separate regions, the Drift Prairie region and the Dissected Till Plains region. The Drift Prairie region is in the north part of this section and has rolling hills and beautiful, natural lakes. The Dissected Till Plains in the southeastern part of this region have soil originally deposited from glaciers.

The Missouri River, the most important river in the state, "cuts" the state in half with the Central Lowlands to the east and the Great Plains to the west. The Great Plains region covers about two-thirds of the western portion of the state. There, gentle hills and plains are broken by rugged rocky features such as ridges, canyons, and buttes. The southwest corner of the state has the dramatic ridges and gullies of the Badlands.

SCOTTS BLUFF NATIONAL MONUMENT

NEBRASKA

Nebraska is a state characterized by plains. In the east, the Dissected Till Plains are drained by the Missouri River. This area of lowlands has many streams and fertile soil, which makes it ideal for agriculture. East of the Dissected Till Plains is the Great Plains region. This region covers most of the state. The land rises gradually from the east to the west over this vast area of flat land.

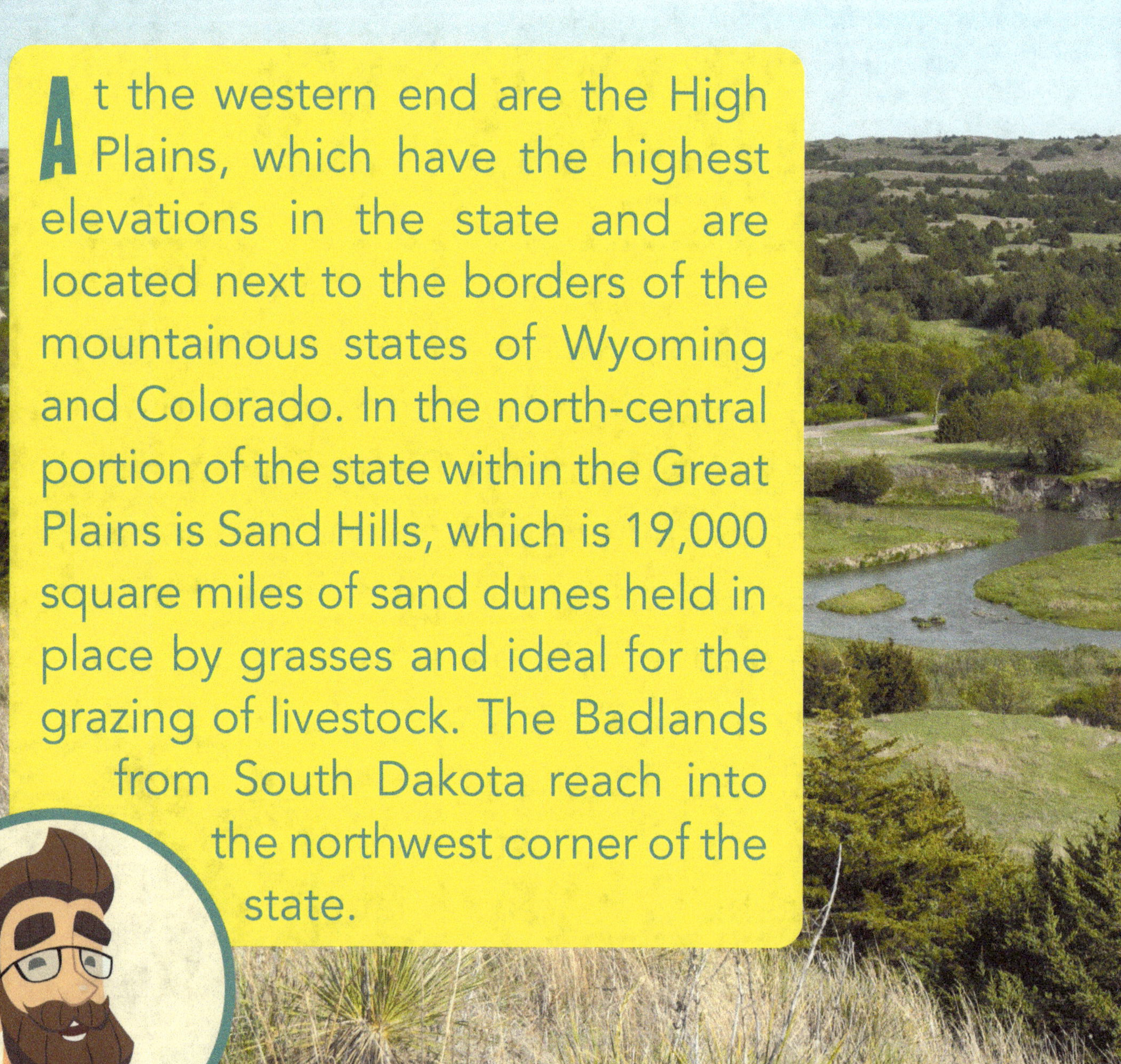

At the western end are the High Plains, which have the highest elevations in the state and are located next to the borders of the mountainous states of Wyoming and Colorado. In the north-central portion of the state within the Great Plains is Sand Hills, which is 19,000 square miles of sand dunes held in place by grasses and ideal for the grazing of livestock. The Badlands from South Dakota reach into the northwest corner of the state.

SANDHILLLS IN NEBRASKA

FLINT HILLS OF KANSAS

KANSAS

The state of Kansas is known for its grasslands. The land elevation rises gradually from east to west across the terrain of Kansas. The Dissected Till Plains, a section of rolling plains with fertile soil, is in the northeast. In the southeastern part of the state, there are the Osage Plains and Flint Hills, which have ridges made from limestone. The Southeastern Plains region has the Arkansas River Lowlands, which cover the state's southeastern corner and have the lowest elevations in the state.

CASTLE ROCK BADLANDS

The central portion of the state is characterized by the Smokey Hills, which have rolling hills with rock formations of sandstone and limestone. The Great Plains region covers the western section of the state. The highest elevations in the state occur in the High Plains part of this region, but none reach over 4,000 feet.

MINNESOTA

Almost all of the state of Minnesota is in the Great Plains region. In the southeastern section is the Driftless Area. It's an area of gently rolling hills with deep river valleys near the Mississippi River. In the southwestern part of the state, the Dissected Tills Plains have fertile soil ideal for farming. The northern part of the state has more variance in its terrain. The Young Drift plains are in the west of this region.

LAKE AGASSIZ

It's a flat, fertile area that is drained by the Red River Valley and is well suited to farming. Much of the terrain in the north-central part of the state was formed by the glaciers of the last major Ice Age. Lake Agassiz was one such large natural lake, but it has drained away over time and is known as the Superior Uplands region today.

There are swamplands, peat bogs, and marshlands in this area as well as the Upper and Lower Red Lake. All of these features are the results of the Ice Age glaciers.

The Mesabi Mountains and the Vermillion Mountains are in the northeast section of the state.

Most of the state of Iowa is part of the Central Plain. This Cornbelt extends across the Midwestern states from Nebraska to Ohio. Of these states, Iowa has the most fertile topsoil. This is especially true of the northern section of the state, which has flat, fertile land perfect for farming. These farming lands are located in the Young Drifts Plains region and many of Iowa's natural lakes are situated there.

FARMS ON A HILLSIDE IN THE IOWA COUNTRYSIDE

FARMLAND LANDSCAPE IN IOWA

At one time, Iowa had many natural wetlands, but most of them have been filled in to create farmlands. The highest point in the state is only 1,670 feet above sea level. In the northeastern section of the state, the Driftless Area region is located near the Mississippi River. Unlike the other Iowa flat farmlands, this area has rough forest-covered hills.

MISSOURI

Above the Missouri River in the northern part of the state lies the Dissected Till Plains region, which is part of the Central Plains region of the US.

The region is characterized by hills and flatlands with fertile, reddish soil for farming. Much of the western part of the state is the Osage Plains region. It's similar to the Dissected Till section, but has soil that isn't as fertile.

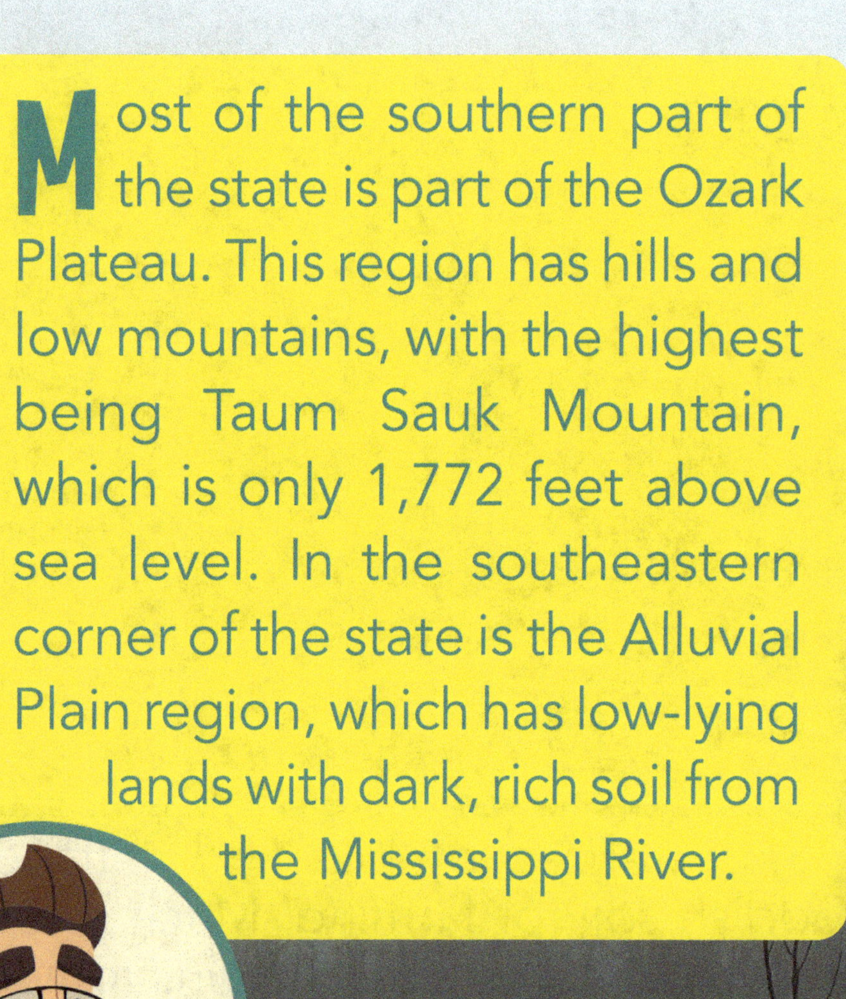

Most of the southern part of the state is part of the Ozark Plateau. This region has hills and low mountains, with the highest being Taum Sauk Mountain, which is only 1,772 feet above sea level. In the southeastern corner of the state is the Alluvial Plain region, which has low-lying lands with dark, rich soil from the Mississippi River.

TAUM SAUK MOUNTAIN FOG

In the southwestern part of the state, the Western Upland region has sandstone and limestone formations. The winding ridges and steep slopes make this area one of the most scenic in the state. Off the shores of Lake Michigan, the Eastern Ridges and Lowlands region has gently rolling hills with rich soil for farming. The Central Plain covers much of the middle of the state. During the last major Ice Age, this area was covered by glaciers.

WISCONSIN DELLS

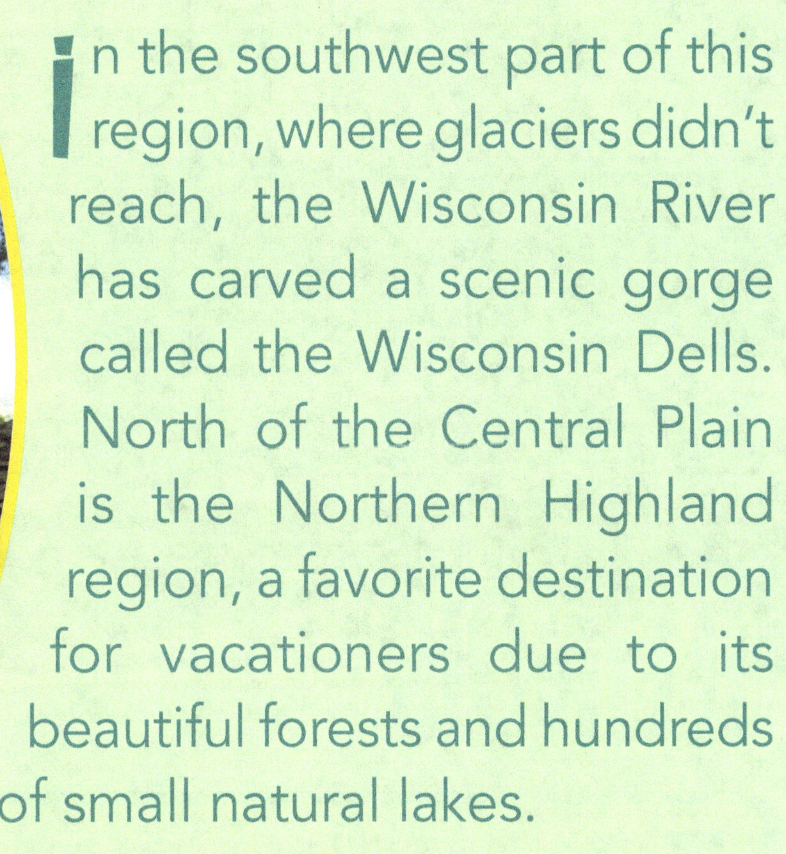

In the southwest part of this region, where glaciers didn't reach, the Wisconsin River has carved a scenic gorge called the Wisconsin Dells. North of the Central Plain is the Northern Highland region, a favorite destination for vacationers due to its beautiful forests and hundreds of small natural lakes.

ILLINOIS

The state of Illinois lies almost completely within the Central Plains. Its rolling hills and rich black soil make it perfect for farming.

The northeastern section of the state, where the city of Chicago is located, is part of the Great Lakes Plains region, which has an elevation just a little higher than sea level.

The center of the state is within the Central Plains and is the agricultural seat of the state, part of the United States farm belt that stretches from the state of Nebraska to the state of Ohio. The northwest corner of the state is part of the Driftless Area region characterized by hills and valleys, although the highest elevation is only 1,235 feet, the peak of Charles Mound. The Shawnee Hills region in the southern part of the state is known for its many orchards.

SHAWNEE NATIONAL FOREST

MICHIGAN

The state of Michigan is two separate landmasses, the Upper Peninsula and the Lower Peninsula. Both are almost entirely covered by the region known as the Great Lakes Plains. The Lower Peninsula is completely located within the Plains.

LAKE IN ALGER COUNTY IN MICHIGAN S UPPER PENINSULA

LAKE ERIE

The eastern section of the Lower Peninsula is a lowland area with some of the lowest elevations statewide, especially in the southeast section along Lake Erie. This region is generally flat and good for agriculture. The western section of the Lower Peninsula as well as its north-central section are more hilly.

GOGEBIC COUNTY, MICHIGAN

The Upper Peninsula's eastern section is within the Great Lakes Plains. It has swampy land that isn't good for farming. The western portion of the Upper Peninsula is the Superior Upland region. It has hilly terrain that has a higher elevation than the rest of the state. In the northern section of the Upper Peninsula there are some low mountain ranges, the Gogebic and the Huron. The highest point is only 1,979 feet at Mount Arvon.

SQUIRE BOON CAVERN, INDIANA

INDIANA

Indiana has several different types of terrain. The Southern Hills and Lowlands have rough hills and valleys with many underground caverns. The state's lowest elevation is also found in the southern section. Most of the rest of the state is located within the Central Plains in the Till Plains region. This area is a fertile area for farming.

WATERFALL IN OWEN COUNTY, INDIANA

Although there are some gentle hills and valleys, for the most part, the land is flat from the glaciers of the last Ice Age, which also deposited minerals making the soil rich. The northwestern section of

the state borders Lake Michigan. It's a low-lying area with rich soil that isn't much higher than sea level. There are large sand dunes separating the coast from the inland land.

OHIO FARMLAND

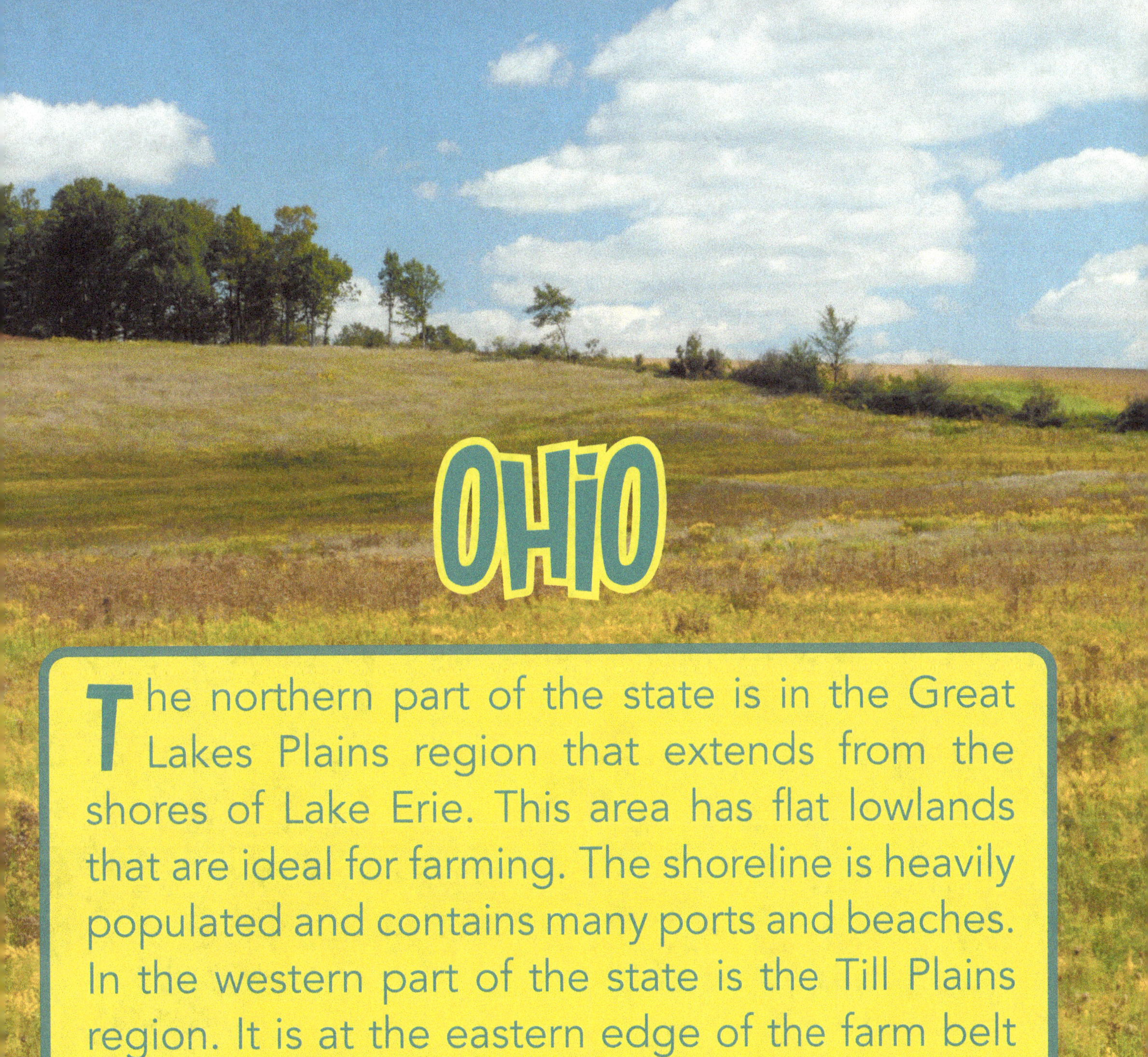

OHIO

The northern part of the state is in the Great Lakes Plains region that extends from the shores of Lake Erie. This area has flat lowlands that are ideal for farming. The shoreline is heavily populated and contains many ports and beaches. In the western part of the state is the Till Plains region. It is at the eastern edge of the farm belt that runs across the entire Midwest.

COAL MINER

This area has rolling hills with the highest elevation being Campbell Hill, which is a height of only 1,549 feet. In the southwest portion of the state, the terrain has a low elevation. It is part of the Bluegrass region that extends into Ohio from the state of Kentucky. The eastern half of the state is in the Allegheny Plateau, which is rugged with deep valleys throughout the rough hills, which are rich with mineral deposits.

SUMMARY

The states of the Midwest are known for their grassland plains and fertile soil.

The Missouri and Mississippi Rivers are important rivers in the Midwest. The scenic Great Lakes are another notable geographic feature in this section of the United States.

Awesome! Now that you've read about the geography of the Midwest section of the United States, you may want to read about the geography of the west in the Baby Professor book *Geography of the US – Western States (California, Arizona, Colorado and More) | Geography for Kids – US States.*

Visit

BABY PROFESSOR
EDUCATION KIDS

www.BabyProfessorBooks.com

to download Free Baby Professor eBooks and view our catalog of new and exciting Children's Books

www.ingramcontent.com/pod-product-compliance
Lightning Source LLC
LaVergne TN
LVHW060827170826
845678LV00010B/1920

* 9 7 9 8 8 6 9 4 3 6 2 0 7 *